thinking divorce?
think again*

*seven realities you need to know

Lorie D. Fowlke, JD

FOWLKEN PRESS

This publication is designed to provide accurate and authoritative information with regard to the subject matter covered. It is sold with the understanding that the publisher and author are not engaged in rendering legal, financial, or other professional advice. If legal services or other expert assistance is required, the services of a competent professional should be sought.

From a Declaration of Principles jointly adopted by a Committee of the American Bar Association and a Committee of Publishers and Associations.

Front cover and book design by Fullnelson Creative. www.fncreative.com
Chapter head illustrations by Lana Grover.

Copyright 2004 by Fowlke and Associates, Inc.
ISBN 0-9743807-0-9

All rights reserved. This book, or parts thereof, may not be reproduced in any form without permission from the author and publisher; exceptions are made for brief excerpts used in published reviews.

Visit us on the Web at:
http://www.thinkingdivorce.com

To Will
who never quit

ACKNOWLEDGEMENTS

I would like to thank all those associates, close friends, and family members who encouraged me to write and finally finish this book. With an ongoing law practice and large family to manage, it was a challenge to complete it. First and foremost I must thank my husband who initially encouraged me to write down the stories and messages he kept hearing from me over the breakfast table. He was also the one who volunteered to do the grocery shopping or fix dinner so I could write in the evenings and on weekends. It was his persistence that brought this idea to fruition.

Thank you to my secretary, Barbara Koepp, my best friend, Dalene Collins, my daughter, Summer Jack, and my sister, Cheryl Karr, who all kindly gave me invaluable feedback when I tentatively shared my first rough draft with them. I greatly appreciate my editor, Elyse Hunter, who reminded me not to mix my metaphors and go easy on the commas. I am grateful to Elizabeth Dalton, J.D. for her mentoring and insight during my years as a family law attorney as well as her enthusiasm for this book and its message. Thanks also to Jane Nelson, of Fullnelson Creative, for her cover design and helpful suggestions.

Finally, I would like to express sincere appreciation to Dr. Stephen Covey, who graciously agreed to write the foreword. His willingness to lend his name and credentials to this project underscores its importance to our society. At some point, we all have to take a stand for what we believe in. These individuals helped make it possible for me to share with you why I have taken my stand on divorce and marriage.

CONTENTS

viii
FOREWORD
by Stephen R. Covey

1
INTRODUCTION

5
PROLOGUE
What Divorce Will Do For You

7
1 - BURNING THROUGH YOUR ASSETS
Divorce Costs "Lotsa" Money

23
2 - YOUR NEW HALF LIFE
Divorce Reduces Your Lifestyle

35
3 - IT ALWAYS HURTS
Divorce Causes Emotional Devastation, Now or Later

47
4 - PERSONAL PAIN DOES NOT STAY HOME
Divorce Negatively Impacts Your Employment

56
5 - "IS IT MY FAULT?"
Divorce Traumatizes Your Children

75
6 - THE MYTH OF BEING FREE
Divorce Complicates Your Life

85
7 - WHERE DID ALL THE PARENTS GO?
Divorce Damages Society

95
DECISION TIME

100
APPENDIX

FOREWORD

by Stephen R. Covey

"When you pick up one end of the stick,
you pick up the other end."

This is an important book. In fact, I suggest it is a "must-read" book for anyone who is seriously considering divorce. As an experienced divorce attorney and a wise and caring person, Lorie Fowlke has done an absolutely needed and masterful job in presenting a balanced and comprehensive picture of "the other end of the stick."

Several years ago, I was on a sabbatical in Hawaii and had a life-changing experience in learning a fundamental principle of life which also directly relates to the divorce decision. I was wandering around the stacks of the library in a very reflective mood and pulled down a book. In it I read three sentences that were so profound and meaningful that they literally staggered me and became the foundation for my work on the 7 Habits. Here are the three sentences:

Between stimulus and response there is a space.
In that space lies our freedom and power to choose our response.
In those choices lie our growth and our happiness.

Notice carefully what it said. Between all that happens to us (stimulus) and our response (decision, action), there is a space. In other words, stimulus and response are not connected. There is a space between them. In that space lies our capacity to think, to pause, to consider the consequences of our response, and finally, to make a decision, to choose our response.

Those choices, those decisions, those actions, will have consequences. If our decisions are unwise, bad consequences will follow. If our decision regarding terminating a marriage is unwise, the consequences could literally be disastrous. I mean really, horribly devastating. Lorie Fowlke, drawing upon her wide and deep experience as a divorce attorney, identifies those consequences (the other end of the stick) in clear and compelling language, illustrating each one with real-life situations and real people with whom she has worked directly.

With animals, there is no space between stimulus and response. They are completely and totally a product of their instincts and/or training and therefore have no ability to reinvent themselves, to choose another path or a higher way. Human beings alone possess this capacity, this special and unique endowment, this space. Only human beings can stop and pause and observe their own involvement and think about the consequences of their actions.

The problem is, when people contemplate divorce, their stressed mental and emotional state drives them into "either/or" thinking: should I get a divorce or should I not? People are also usually so full of self-justification and a spirit of victimism and accusation that they simply fall into the animal "fight or flight" approach to stress. Stimulus and response then become inseparable. There is no space. They literally abandon their human endowment of self-awareness, of self-reflection. They begin to define winning as beating. The only alternative they see to this win/lose approach is lose/win, or martyrdom, which by then they are sick and tired of taking anyway.

This whole fight (active or passive) or flight (divorce) is compounded by the wider culture that sees divorce as an acceptable, if not a desirable, alternative to marital conflict or simply marital numbness. It's therefore becoming more and more common, even epidemic. Sympathetic friends and colluding loved ones who join in finding or interpreting evidence against the offending spouse also nourish the divorce decision. They massage one another's hearts. Any discussion about a possible third alternative, other than fight or flight, is seen as giving in, capitulating and continuing to lose. They abandon their human self-reflective endowments as well, and a social conspiracy is often formed, justifying the divorce decision.

Remember, that which a person most earnestly desires, he or she most easily believes. When an offended spouse simply wants out, wants relief, wants some peace, some space, some respect, some self-esteem, then they easily believe that divorce is the answer. And sometimes divorce is the best answer. Lorie Fowlke has been around the block so many times she knows full well that there are justifiable reasons for divorce. But she also beautifully illustrates the seven huge consequences that inevitably follow such a decision and why they must be thought about carefully and in depth so that principles and wisdom, rather than naiveté and foolish hope, win the day.

If you are considering divorce and debating whether you want to give this book a serious read, just read the short introduction and the final chapter, called "Decision Time," which is only three pages long. In it the author cites scientific studies that have shown that two-thirds of unhappily married people who remained married reported that their marriages were happy five years later. Even 80% of those who rated their marriages as "very unhappy" said that they were happily married five years later. Let me quote Lorie's own words: "The most startling statistics in this study show that if a couple is unhappy, the chances of their being happy five years later is 64% if they remain together, but only 19% if they divorce and remarry." Lorie told me, "Studies show that divorce does not make people happier, yet families are impacted for generations."

The thing that will go through you like osmosis as you read this book is that you do have control over your decisions and actions, but you do not have control over the consequences. They are controlled by natural laws, by principles. If you decide that divorce is the only way out of the "hell you're in," be prepared to be powerfully, negatively affected—economically, emotionally and in your whole lifestyle. Perhaps worst of all is the impact upon the children, both short- and long-term, in their own ability and capacity to make and keep commitments and to sustain the inevitable rigors of an interdependent marriage.

I know many will say, "Yes, but all of those bad things are not as bad as the situation I'm in now." This may be the case and may justify a divorce decision. But it may not be the case if you have not thoroughly examined what those consequences may really be.

Nevertheless, you may be hurt and frustrated and justified. What then can be done? Lorie basically brings out that if people were to expend the same effort, energy, resources and creativity on improving themselves and their marriages that they do in fighting and flighting strategies and the divorce process, they could find third alternative solutions.

Of course it would take great patience, great endurance and great courage. One would need to redefine love as a verb instead of a feeling, and use the space between stimulus and response to perform acts of love that will restore or heal the relationship.

It is a well-established principle that the best way to change another is to change yourself. This is an "inside-out" approach. The world basically teaches "outside in" for problem solving: "Others must change. Circumstances must change." The inside-out approach is painstaking and often "culturally incorrect," but experience with relationships has proven it to be the only solution that truly lasts. Sometimes for various reasons, it won't work either—it may not salvage a marriage. But at least you go out knowing you tried your best, maintained your integrity and didn't get sucked into a cycle of self-justification, victimism and an incessant need for external validation.

I remember a man visiting with me one time about his unhappiness in his marriage. He basically said that the feeling was no longer there, that both of them felt the same way, and that neither saw any hope for the future. But he was very worried about its impact upon their three children and asked for my counsel. After listening for quite a while, I said to him, "Love her." And he said, "Well, as I told you, the feeling isn't there anymore." I said, "I heard that. Love her." He asked, "How do you love when you don't love?" I replied, "Where do you get the idea that love is a feeling? Love is a verb. It's Hollywood that has dramatized love as a feeling." If you study any of the great and enduring literature that has sustained the great institutions of society, like the family, you will discover that love is always referred to as a verb. It is something you do. It is the love you give. It is the sacrifice you make, the service you give. Love the feeling is the fruit of love the verb. It's like the mother who goes into "the valley of the shadow" in bringing forth a child that creates the feeling of love. Again, love the feeling is the fruit of love the verb. We have control over the action, and if we consistently maintain the action of love, eventually the feeling of love can be restored.

Too idealistic? Perhaps. But perhaps not. I have found that deep in their hearts, most people know there's a great deal they can do to improve themselves and thus to improve a relationship. There are so many different kinds of deposits they can put into what we could call an Emotional Bank Account of another. Admittedly, this takes a different mindset and a different skill set, but these things are learnable, particularly when you think about the magnitude of the issues at stake.

Finally, the interesting perspective of this book, in contrast to the various anti-divorce books by therapists and social scientists, is that it comes from a very practical and legal perspective. It comes from a person in the divorce business who has continual first-hand experience with its consequences. Lorie is a person of integrity and wisdom who would love to work herself out of a job.

Henry David Thoreau taught, "There are a thousand hacking at branches of evil to one striking at the root." I believe Lorie is striking at the root.

INTRODUCTION

I am a divorce attorney. Like any good attorney, let me begin this book with a disclaimer. The purpose of this book is not to make any individual feel guilty or to preclude victims of abuse from seeking a divorce when it is appropriate. I had a client whose spouse killed himself (he "showed her"). Another client's spouse tried to kill her (she "deserved it"). There were some whose relationships were poison, with at least one of the spouses unwilling to change. There was little doubt these people needed a divorce and I was glad I could help them. However, there have been other situations where I've been convinced that if a couple directed the time, money and energy they spent on divorce litigation toward re-establishing their relationship and saving their marriage, a family would be salvaged. I have seen incredible problems overcome. It took a lot of work, proper motivation, and consistent commitment by both spouses, but the rewards were worth it to the families involved.

Everyone knows divorce is epidemic in our society. We started with a culture where women were property and divorce was unthinkable. Later, people often endured a bad marriage but could get divorced for a good reason or "grounds". Currently, it appears any problem, conflict, or loss of passion is frequently addressed by divorce. And business is booming!

Some people appear more justified than others in seeking a divorce. Those who are victims of physical abuse, abandoned by adultery, or have an unresolved conflict in values may have legitimate and necessary reasons to divorce. People seek divorces for all sorts of other reasons, as well, including the catchall "mental cruelty" or, in many states, "irreconcilable differences". Some individuals are worn down by conflict--that non-stop arguing and constant bickering that drives one crazy. There may be an imbalance of power. This is generally manifested by a lack of respect, with one spouse passive and one always in control. Some people are just generally dissatisfied with their spouse. This is often based upon unrealistic expectations of each other, or of marriage in general. A spouse may also be dissatisfied due to the fact that some other person appears more attractive; in those cases the unsatisfactory spouse is in a no-win situation, since every little slight will be magnified by their partner to justify their choice to leave.

Divorce may not always be the solution you anticipate. In fact, it often creates new problems. It is not my intent here to judge whether or not someone should get a divorce. No one can do that for another person. I just want people to think about it a little harder and realize it may not be the remedy they expect. When someone's life is full of problems, it is a myth to believe that the other side of a divorce will bring the solutions.

When I first started practicing law, my mentor, an older gentleman who was of retirement age but still going full steam, advised me that most lawsuits, including divorce, were based in either selfishness or greed. Of course, it only takes one side with these characteristics to start a case. A lawsuit is often long, arduous, miserable, and expensive for everyone. In family law litigation, these characteristics aggravate an already difficult emotional process and can create a nightmare for everyone involved. Many domestic relations attorneys become burned out in this area of practice as they watch people who once loved each other cross the fine line from love to hate and act out their anger at their former spouse. Attorneys muse that divorces are the only cases where you know the opposing parties have been intimate. Family therapists have told me the opposite of love is not hate, but indifference. I rarely see indifference in my practice.

This book is not intended to be a legal treatise for attorneys, or even a sophisticated review for therapists or other professionals. It is an easy-to-read, practical guide to the consequences of a divorce in today's culture. I want people in our society to recognize the real life practical effects of their choice to obtain a divorce *before* the damage is inflicted. Hopefully, some of you will heed the caution implicit in these pages and seek a different avenue to address your problems. I am not claiming to be the country's expert on divorce, but there are some things most divorce lawyers know. That is the information in this book. I just happened to write it down.

PROLOGUE

Several years ago, "Leslie" asked me to lunch. I had not seen her for quite a while, and realized it had been longer than I thought when she confessed, over bagels and salmon cream cheese, that she had had an affair. By then it was over and she was trying to put everything back together. But things were not working out. It was difficult. She was bored with her job. She was stressed trying to balance kids and work. Her husband was having a hard time forgiving her, though he claimed he wanted to stay married, and she just was not having any "fun". She had decided to seek a divorce. What did I think?

As a general rule, I have learned not to reveal my inner thoughts. Since I have never been known for my tact, I usually end up putting my foot in my mouth. People do not really want to know.

"No, I really want to know," Leslie insisted. I suspected she had little idea of what going through a divorce would be like. The best way to help her, I decided, would be to tell her just what to expect. Then she could decide for herself.[1]

---

[1] *Last time I heard from Leslie, she was still working on her marriage. It was not always easy but she was happy most of the time.*

I told Leslie what I am telling you. If you are considering a divorce, take time to reconsider before moving forward. While reconsidering, become aware of what a divorce will actually mean to you and your family. There are seven major reasons I believe a divorce may not be a constructive resolution to your problems. If you go through this list and still feel divorce is the right answer for you, at least you have done your homework, and, hopefully, your new problems will be more manageable.

1

BURNING THROUGH YOUR ASSETS

Divorce Costs "Lotsa" Money

RACE FOR CONTROL OF THE ASSETS

PAY THE BILLS IN THE MEANTIME

GET A GOOD ATTORNEY

PAY EXPENSES OF THE PROCESS

If you want to get a divorce, you must think about money. While it is obviously not the most important thing in life, it is essential to successfully survive the divorce process. When you separate from your spouse, your living expenses will still exist. On a temporary basis, you may not have access to your share of the marital assets, particularly if your spouse makes it to the bank before you do. Your half of the joint bank account may be gone, at least temporarily. You will be told that eventually you will get it back, but it could take months before you get into court to have a judge address the issue. Meanwhile, you still need to pay the mortgage or rent, utilities, groceries, and car bills and maintenance. It is very frustrating, but the world (and bill collectors) will not stay on hold while you go through this emotional and legal crisis.

Once you figure out how you are going to physically survive, you need money to obtain a good attorney. No matter what it takes, you should get a good attorney. Never underestimate this. Most people do not know if they have a good attorney or not, at least not at first. Sometimes they do not know afterwards, either. Typically, if an attorney returns calls, keeps clients informed of what is going on in the case, and sounds intelligent at a court hearing, people are satisfied that their attorney is competent.

While these are good things to see, they may not guarantee your attorney really knows what is going on, or, better yet, knows how to get you what you want, need, or are entitled to.

Law practice is kind of like medicine these days in that everyone is specialized. You want an attorney who concentrates on family law or domestic relations. While you can look in the yellow pages, call the state bar association or talk to your friends for referrals, the best way to find a good attorney is to ask other attorneys. Which attorney do other attorneys refer clients to when they are too busy or cannot take the case? Call some local law offices and ask for names of the best domestic attorneys in town. Soon you will hear the same names repeatedly. One of those names is the attorney you want.

This attorney you select will want money. Unlike medicine, most attorneys, if they have practiced very long, require a substantial retainer before they start working on your case. The good attorneys in town have been around long enough to hear every sob story you can come up with to explain why you cannot afford this, and they will usually stand firm on this issue. This is because they have probably been burned early in their career and now know that if they do not get the money up front, they may not get it at all. The only thing attorneys have to sell is their time. Most attorneys are honest about keeping track of the time they spend on your case, but be aware there are a few who do not bill accurately. Their reputation usually precedes them. A good attorney is worth every penny you give them. By the same token, you can waste a lot of money on a bad one, and lose a lot of other things as well. Do not scrimp on this. Beg, borrow, or do whatever it takes to accomplish retaining a good attorney if you do go ahead with a divorce. It could make all the difference in how you live your life and what you have to live it with when the divorce is over.

Besides living expenses and a good attorney, you will need money for court costs, filing fees, service of subpoenas, and other expenses associated with discovery, which is the process of legally collecting information for your case. There could also be fees for all types of experts, depending on the nature of the issues in dispute; those include accountants, appraisers, Realtors, therapists, custody evaluators, special masters, and mediators, to name a few. Failure to come up with the money needed for these expenses could jeopardize your case. The fact that few people have this kind of money at their disposal is irrelevant to the process or the results.

Don

"Don"[2] came into the lawyer's office because his wife, "Lisa," had served him with a divorce complaint. He did not want a divorce, but she was adamant that she wanted to move on with her life. Don had been out of work for many months but had earned a little extra income by doing odd mechanical jobs in the shop, a shed he owned some distance from the house. Lisa worked as a sales representative for a vacuum cleaner manufacturer. She traveled quite a bit and was the primary breadwinner for the family. While she was bringing in the bacon, Don was cleaning the house and providing the primary care for their three young children, though Lisa also helped with the kids.

Don was heartbroken about the divorce and the fact that Lisa had basically kicked him out of the house. He was concerned about the children and who was helping them with their homework. Lisa considered Don a leech who would never amount to anything since he never earned

[2] All stories are true with names and some identifying facts changed to protect anonymity.

much money or kept a job for any substantial length of time. Lisa assumed that because she was the mom she would keep the kids and Don would be the one to move out. Don did not like it, but he also assumed that was the way it would be.

After meeting with a lawyer, Don discovered he would be a good candidate for being the custodial parent since he had been the children's primary caregiver, a prime factor in that determination. However, Lisa would never agree to such an arrangement, which meant a court fight, which, in turn, meant money--lots of it. Most family law attorneys charge the largest retainer for divorces when a custody battle is included. For Don, this meant he had to come up with the money to initially retain the lawyer. He also needed money to pay for a custody evaluation, a process where child psychologists or social workers interview everyone involved, frequently administer psychological tests, and make a recommendation to the court for the placement of the children. Often this costs several thousand dollars, and the lawyer and psychologist want the money up front.

Don did not have the money to pay his bills, let alone hire an expensive attorney or pay for a custody evaluation. He also did not have the emotional stamina for even an initial hearing to determine temporary custody. In spite of legal advice to the contrary, Don believed that somehow things would work out the way they were supposed to. He paid the minimal amount to his attorney to get through the divorce process with a minimum of fuss. Lisa hired an aggressive divorce attorney, got control of the marital assets and the children, gave a pittance to Don and allowed him minimum visitation with the children. Years later, Don went to see another lawyer to try and "undo" some of the effects of the decree but discovered that it is twice as hard as doing it right the first time. The results of litigation are frequently not perceived as fair. Participating in the court process without the money to secure adequate counsel and necessary experts was like doing battle with one arm tied behind his back.

With a good attorney and funds to work through the process, it is likely Don could have been awarded custody of the children, possession of the marital home, and alimony to help meet his expenses, along with child support. Instead, he spent years living in the shop and seeing his kids whenever Lisa felt like it, since she knew he would not take her to court for failure to follow the visitation rules. By the way, no one formally involved in the judicial process ever addressed how the children fared without their dad around.

Debbie

Debbie had been married for 24 years. Her husband, Jack had always handled all the money and financial transactions in their marriage. He had been physically and verbally abusive to her and the children but had such tight control over everyone that no one ever thought of making a public complaint. When the children were grown, Debbie finally got the nerve to file for a divorce. She had put aside a little money for a retainer; however, Jack refused to agree to anything. Everything required a court hearing. He was upset Debbie had left him and he was not going to let her go without a fight.

Both Debbie and Jack had good attorneys. They scheduled a series of meetings to try to come up with an agreement; however, when it came time to putting anything they discussed down on paper, Jack always changed his mind. He was convinced that if he kept stalling long enough Debbie would either give up the idea of the divorce, or give up her demands for alimony. Jack knew

Debbie was running out of money and he had access to much more cash than she did.

Debbie was getting frustrated and also knew she was running out of money. Her attorney was doing great, but insisted on being paid as they went along. Fortunately for Debbie, she had a neighbor who was very supportive. He and his wife decided to advance funds for Debbie's litigation to ensure she received a fair settlement. Ultimately, Jack and Debbie resolved most of the terms of the divorce and went to trial over alimony. Debbie received an award of alimony that will enable her to stay in her home and support herself. Her budget is trimmed down from what it used to be, but she can pay her bills.

If you decide to proceed with a divorce, find the resources to survive through the divorce process and obtain a good attorney. Then, use those resources wisely. Once you have decided to go through with a divorce, hopefully you and your spouse will make some decisions, on a temporary basis, to keep the bills paid and household running until a final division can be agreed upon or court ordered. If you and your spouse cannot even communicate to this degree, seek legal counsel immediately. A court will provide temporary orders to accomplish this task until a final decision is made. Keep in mind, states differ significantly in how this process is done and what you are entitled to in the interim.

When you have met with an attorney, learn to ask questions and find out how the system works. Understand that most attorneys charge by the minute, so if they give you materials to read, read them, and you may find answers to your questions. If they make staff available to help you, use their help. Staff time is always cheaper than the attorney's time. If the attorney gives you advice, listen to it, and consider it very carefully before rejecting it. Always, always, always be completely honest and up front with your attorney. He or she can minimize problem areas or do damage control if necessary if they know the facts, but if they are surprised in court, their ability to help you is limited. It was a real shock to me when I discovered that many people lie to their attorney, or do not tell the whole truth about relevant facts. Many attorneys routinely put a clause in their retainer agreement or contract, which provides that they can withdraw from your case if you misrepresent the facts to them or fail to abide by the court orders. I call it the "pay—obey—or go away" clause.

I will never forget when I was in court vigorously pursuing my client's right to have visitation with his eight-year-old daughter. The mother had been routinely denying visitation for months. Mom was claiming Dad was a "wacko" and the child was not safe with him. "Absolutely untrue," I protested vehemently to the judge. Imagine my surprise when opposing counsel pulled out a newspaper clipping from the local community press identifying my client as having been arrested a few months before for domestic violence, a fact my client had neglected to mention during our interview in preparation for the hearing. He decided it was not important because the charges were later dismissed and it was all based upon a misunderstanding with his wife. If I had known that before the hearing, I could have been the one to bring it up or been prepared to respond when it was raised. As it was, I was unprepared, to say the least. We still got the visitation, but it was not as liberal as it should have been, and Mom received no sanctions for denying the visits in the past. The only thing worse than not coming up with the money for competent counsel is to manage to scrape it together and then fail to seek the attorney's advice or follow their instructions.

What do you get for all this money? You must remember that attorneys are not therapists or ecclesiastical leaders, though clients often want to use them as such. I always tell my clients they are not paying me for therapeutic advice and when they seek it from me they are wasting their money. The attorney's goal is to get your property and debts divided, resolve the issues about custody and support, and get the process completed as quickly as possible. The court process typically views a divorce like the dissolution of a business partnership. The court's function is to complete fact-finding and legal analysis, and, while individual judges may recognize the presence of the emotional trauma and devastation of the parties, there is little they can do about it in that forum. Attorneys are counselors at law but they are not social workers.

While most people want the situation resolved quickly, the court process is not swift. Courts rarely address the problems that cause the ongoing conflict; they just impose a solution. The problems continue. The judge must make a decision based upon readily identifiable and objective criteria. In most states there are now laws allowing no fault divorce, which means the judge will not be concerned with the reasons behind the divorce. The reasons for the divorce rarely have any impact on the division of property, debts, support or custody. However, the reasons for the divorce may often be exactly what is driving the litigation for the parties themselves. Without addressing them, the problems and litigation and attendant costs can go on indefinitely.

Because divorce court retains jurisdiction over everyone so long as support and custody are issues, ongoing litigation is almost guaranteed if the underlying problems leading to the divorce are not addressed and resolved, at least to some extent. Some cases go on for years. Some continue until all the children are grown, all the money is gone and there is literally nothing more to fight about. This leads to another divorce attorneys' maxim: A client for a divorce is a client for life. While many people blame the lawyers, the court process itself is simply not designed to allow the parties to deal with the "emotional garbage" that created the problem in the first place.

Giving such a large chunk of your hard earned money to a lawyer for your divorce pays for this litigation process.

The American court system is a great improvement over violence, but it was not created to address these types of problems. Most attorneys would acknowledge that litigation is a cumbersome form of communication. Some attorneys believe that the courtroom is not the proper forum for family law issues to be resolved. It makes bitter enemies and destroys relationships with the very people you once loved the most.

Many state court systems have made advancements in recognizing this dilemma and either mandate or encourage different forms of alternative dispute resolution including mediation, arbitration, or collaborative law. These processes do much more to address the underlying basis for the conflict and often help the parties move forward with their lives. It usually costs less as well. However, it only takes one of the two parties to sabotage this procedure. The basic premise that I repeat over and over is this: either you come to an agreement or someone else decides. The longer the two of you fight, the more it will cost. The more decisions you leave to the judge, the more frustrated you may be, since a judge will never know the situation as well as you do and has limited discretion to creatively resolve your dispute. Frequently, they are given facts based on a "he said—she said" scenario, and, in an endeavor to be fair, split the proverbial baby in half. Many judges believe, in domestic litigation, if both sides are unhappy, the court must have made the right decision.

If you are contemplating a divorce, be financially prepared. You should be trying to get out of debt and putting money aside to pay for these anticipated expenses. This money could be spent on educating your children, paying for therapy or learning better communication skills. If you think you will come through a divorce without spending money, usually "lotsa'" money, think again.

2

YOUR NEW HALF LIFE

Divorce Reduces Your Lifestyle

**ONE HOUSEHOLD CANNOT DIVIDE INTO
TWO HOUSEHOLDS WITH THE SAME INCOME**

CHILDREN NOW HAVE TWO HOMES

BANKS DO NOT CARE ABOUT YOUR DIVORCE

DEBTS DO NOT DISAPPEAR

It is fairly obvious arithmetic that you cannot divide one household into two households with the same amount of income and live the same lifestyle. Most states provide for an equitable division of the assets and property. This property includes real property (land, buildings, homes) and personal property (bank accounts, furniture, retirement accounts, vehicles, bikes, camping equipment, and virtually everything else accumulated during the marriage). Under some limited circumstances the court may also re-distribute property you had before the marriage or accumulated after your separation.

Often one parent will keep more of the property belonging to the children if the children have a primary residence with that parent. However, the children will still need a place to sleep and keep their clothes when visiting the other parent. The living expenses for the same number of people are nearly doubled, as now there are two residences requiring rent and utilities. Instead of two people on one homeowners or car insurance policy, there are two separate policies. You need two dining room tables now and two sets of kitchenware, two master bedrooms and two closets.

Frequently there is a home that has equity that must be divided between the two spouses. This may mean selling the house so that the mortgage can be paid off and the equity divided. Then both spouses have half as much money to start over again, and half the income with which to qualify for a new home mortgage. If children are involved, a court may order, or the parties sometimes agree, that the custodial parent can keep the house until the children are grown or until that spouse remarries before having to pay the other spouse their share of equity. Some courts allow this arrangement for the stability of the children. However, that places a real burden on the non-custodial spouse, since he or she has to wait, sometimes for years, before receiving their share of equity and therefore having the money to start over.

For the parent staying in the home, it may be difficult to find a way to repay the other parent's share of equity when the time comes, so frequently this requires selling the home, sooner or later. This is one reason the poverty statistics are so high for women and children, since once the house is lost, many women who have been homemakers during the marriage do not have the marketable skills to obtain jobs with sufficient earning potential to qualify for another home mortgage on their own.

Besides the division of assets and multiplication of expenses, a divorce often means a loss of "home life" which cannot always be quantified. The marriage is always a partnership of some sort, whether it functions well or not. Usually the tasks involved in keeping a home have been divided to some extent between the spouses. While many times one spouse is more involved than the other, there is still usually some assistance by the second adult in the home. After the divorce this assistance and support is gone. You must now be the one to complete all household tasks with no help from a spouse. One person must do all the maintenance of cars and house. All the grocery shopping, lawn care, garbage duty, home repairs, homework help, cleaning, cooking, laundry, and so forth are now one person's responsibility. When added to the work involved in keeping a regular job and possibly caring for children as well, life becomes more stress than fun.

Besides the loss of someone who may or may not have helped around the house and yard, there is the loss of what I call the family spirit. While some spouses consider this a blessing, it will be a change in the home. As much as you hate it, the kids will often feel this difference and be affected by it. Unless the home was filled with physical violence or conflict, this loss will leave a void of some type. What you replace it with may be better, but it may not. For example, if you used to have a weekly night for a family activity, it will not feel the same. If both parents were at least somewhat involved in disciplining the kids or providing feedback, this will change. Even though the hope is that both parents will remain involved in working with the children, it will be different. It is naïve to disregard this consequence; it is better to recognize it for what it is and deal with it in some fashion.

Paul

Paul's wife Jenny decided to file for divorce when she discovered Paul was gay. They had four children and it was a difficult decision, but she could not deal with the issue any other way. Paul was relieved that she finally took a position and he could get out of the marriage. However, the finances were not in good shape, due in part, to some problems Paul had at work. There were large credit card balances and the mortgage was at risk.

Jenny was a musician who performed and gave lessons, which meant her income was irregular at best. Paul had a good job, but it was in jeopardy due to some unauthorized trips to Las Vegas at company expense. At the court hearing for temporary support, the judge ordered Paul to maintain most of the debts while everything was sorted out. With the burden of child support, Paul did not have enough money to go around. The mortgage payments became later and later, credit card interest accumulated with alarming speed, and Paul did not pay all the support he was ordered to pay, which also put him at risk for a contempt citation from the court.

Jenny was not interested in contempt. She wanted the bills paid so she could get on with her life. She started to work full time in addition to the performing and teaching music lessons. Paul spent his extra time out of town with friends because he was lonely without the kids. The kids missed Mom and Dad, but managed reasonably well since there was a minimum of conflict. Eventually, Paul and Jenny decided to cash in the retirement they had accumulated, to pay the bills. Paul lost most of his equity in the house to make up for the support he owed and everyone's savings were, of course, depleted.

Susan

Susan had been married to Joe for five years when she finally realized it was not going to get better. Joe had been in the military for four of their five years together, bringing in a regular paycheck. However, Joe's idea of a marriage included drinking with his buddies every night and slapping Susan around a little if she objected too much. They had one daughter and Susan had stayed home since she was born. As soon as Susan and Joe agreed to get a divorce, Joe re-directed the direct deposit from his pay check to a separate checking account in his name only. He gave Susan no money and no access to the family car.

Susan and her baby moved in with her parents and the rest of her family in another state. She got a job and enrolled in college. She soon discovered the dilemma of the working poor. She made too much money to qualify for Medicaid and welfare, but not enough to support herself and her child. She spent the next two years living with her parents so she could finish school.

The court awarded Susan enough child support and alimony to allow her to live on her own, when added to her job earnings. But, Joe rarely paid. Susan's attorney and the State Office of Child Support collection brought Joe into court six times before the court did more than hold him in contempt and assess fines and attorneys fees against him, which he never paid. A year and a half after they separated, the court actually sentenced Joe to 30 days in jail. That finally got his attention and the support started to come regularly, as ordered.

For Susan, living at her parents' was a real challenge. She appreciated their support, of course, but it was difficult after having her own apartment for five years. For the first year she and her daughter even had to share a bedroom until her brother finally left for college and she got her own room back. But it is true that two women cannot share the same kitchen very easily, and while most of the time she was glad her Mom was around, there were times when she would have almost considered going back to the abuse, just to have her own place.

In planning for a divorce, you must recognize that your lifestyle and standard of living will probably change. You should prepare for this consequence as well as you can. Depending on your personal situation, you may want to save money, collect good used furniture, check out available public resources and decide on a way to help your children understand the upcoming changes. Be aware that everything accumulated before the divorce, including during your separation, may be counted as a marital asset to be divided with your spouse.

If divorce means that you will need more education or training to take care of yourself, discover what career skills will be necessary. Investigate the local educational or vocational institutions to discover what options are available and what they will cost. Sometimes grants are offered to "displaced homemakers" or are offered in certain areas of study. Learn how much time it will take to achieve the ability to be self-supporting.

Sometimes a divorce means you will lose a spouse who has been supportive in your particular business or job. If this spouse is someone who will have to be replaced, be prepared to finance that replacement and find someone with the necessary skills.

You should be looking for a place to live and possibly collecting basic furniture with which you feel comfortable. Pay off your debts as much as possible. There are many divorces where the only real dispute is who is going to take which debt. In that division, be aware that third party creditors are not bound by your divorce decree. This means that if Kimberly takes the Tahoe and is supposed to make the payments under the terms of the divorce decree, the bank does not care. John's name is on the loan and the bank will come after John if the payments are not made, regardless of the terms of the divorce.

In this situation Kimberly might not make the payments. She also might let the insurance lapse and let the car loan go into default. The bank will obtain the necessary insurance to protect its asset and eventually repossess and sell the car, leaving a deficiency judgment, meaning the car could be sold for less than the money owed on the loan. The bank will come after John for the deficiency, including the cost of the insurance. If Kimberly remarried, had no job and no assets in her name, John could be stuck with the judgment. He may not be able to pay it, and eventually he could file for bankruptcy. Of course, he will bankrupt out of his attorneys fees, as well, so he will not feel too guilty. This is another reason attorneys' fee retainers keep going up.

The best way to resolve this dilemma is to assign debts to the party in whose name the loans are held. If that is not possible, be aware of the problems and ask your attorney for creative solutions to address the possibility that the other party will not pay their assigned debt.

Do not take your lifestyle for granted. It involves not only the money that comes into the household, but the atmosphere of the home itself. Be aware that your perception of this atmosphere is just that, i.e., your perception. The perception of your spouse and your children may be quite different, based upon their own needs and desires. Consider carefully the positive and negative impact on that home atmosphere before proceeding with a divorce. If you think a divorce will not significantly impact your lifestyle, and that of your family, think again.

3

IT ALWAYS HURTS

*Divorce Causes
Emotional Devastation,
Now or Later*

PAIN LEADING TO THE DIVORCE

PAIN THROUGHOUT THE DIVORCE PROCESS

PROLONGING THE PAIN

HEALING THE PAIN

There are few people who escape some level of emotional trauma when going through a divorce. The pain is on at least two levels. There is pain associated with whatever brought you or your partner to the point of seeking the divorce, and there is the trauma of the divorce process itself.

DIVORCE PAIN

Few people marry with the idea that they will not make it last the rest of their lives. To come to the point in a relationship where you have to acknowledge that either you made a mistake or things changed is difficult for almost everyone. No matter how sure you are that divorce is the right course of action for you, there will usually be a loss. In a way, the loss is more painful than a spouse's death. You must not only deal with the absence of that spouse, as you do when they die, but now you face the end of your dreams as well. People handle this in a variety of ways, but few come out unscathed. Even in a short marriage, the pain of the "failure" will always be with you along with whatever uncertainty or other emotional baggage accompanies it.

Often, the degree of trauma in a divorce may hinge on whether you are the leaver or the left, though both suffer to some degree. Everyone experiences some level of grief because a divorce does represent such a significant loss. If you are the one who decided to leave, you could be frustrated because of the situation in which you now find yourself. You may have been dealing with a lot of grief, anger, or pain for a very long time. It could be primarily the fault of the other spouse or you could be the one who wants to leave for a variety of reasons. Even though the divorce may be your choice, it still represents pain at some level.

If you are the one who is left, the news that your spouse is going to seek a divorce may be devastating. Frequent emotions are anger or despair. This may come as a shock or it may be the culmination of ongoing threats for years. Either way, it is a crazy time, and healing will be a time-consuming, agonizing, and stressful process. You may constantly be asking yourself, "why?"

People living in pain usually strike out at those around them. They wound each other, causing more pain, and a cycle is created. Both of you will experience a loss of intimacy that you may not have anticipated. In fact, a number of couples seem to have real difficulty disconnecting. Because of the anger, pain and/or grief they are experiencing, some people evolve into a kind of "negative intimacy". They use every excuse to prick and poke at the divorcing spouse, almost as if letting go is the ultimate tragedy, the ultimate loss, and they are not yet ready to face it. Because divorce lawsuits are cases where the opposing parties have been sexually intimate, the closeness these people have shared makes them more vulnerable to attack from their spouse. Many people suffer greatly. Only after they reach an attitude of indifference, can the healing truly begin.

I have observed few gender differences in the reaction to this trauma. The differences in reaction are based more upon which spouse is the perceived abuser or victim, controller or passive participant, leaver or left. However, I have noticed that women are often the spouses who are physically abused. This may correlate with the phenomenon I see of more women who tend to be passive-aggressive. I find men are often the spouses who are clueless when the other spouse leaves. They sit in my office and report, "I knew there were some problems, but I did not think she was serious."

Either husband or wife can be the victim of verbal abuse, and frequently it can be both. Besides the ongoing conflict created by verbal abuse, it is symptomatic of many other problems in the relationship, originating, I believe, in a basic lack of respect for the other person. This is not going to change as you go through the divorce process. Many individuals act surprised or frustrated when their spouse resorts to name-calling and demeaning demands. I have to remind them there is no reason to expect the nature of the relationship or the personality of the persons involved to change because of the divorce process; in fact it usually gets worse.

PROCESS PAIN

Obtaining a divorce through the courts is a process guaranteed to make a bad situation much worse before it gets better. The court system is adversarial, based upon the principle that the search for truth will provide the judge with adequate information to make the best decision. Rather than assisting you and your spouse to find constructive, equitable, and creative ways to divide your property and share your children, in court each side will advocate what is in their own best interests, and leave the other side to advance their point of view. The theory is the judge will find a solution somewhere in the middle that meets both parties' needs. If you were able to communicate with your spouse in a somewhat constructive manner at the beginning of the process, it is likely that will disappear for a long time after a few court hearings in which you sit at opposite tables and hear your attorneys denigrate each of you. Some states have a special family court that is a little better in handling these types of cases, but it is still adversarial. Again, as I keep telling my clients, either you come to an agreement or we go to court and the judge decides. While most judges try to be fair, in the win-lose scenario of a courtroom, at least one of you, and often both of you, will be unhappy with the result.

Our society has begun to recognize that this process is not only difficult for the couple, but the children as well. It prolongs the necessary healing that must take place and, many times, imbeds the parties in a bitterness from which they never recover. Now, many states require people to participate in various types of alternative dispute resolution to address the issues in a divorce before they can go to court. These processes allow you to have much more input into the final resolution. You learn to compromise, but you may still pick and choose those things you feel most strongly about. No one knows the two of you better than the two of you. That can make it more difficult, since you know how to trigger each other and push each other's buttons. However, with a neutral party to help keep the lines of communication open and on a positive note, so much as possible, it is more likely you will both come to a resolution that is acceptable. You can do this with much less anger and emotional drain than coming back to the courthouse every few months for a win-lose decision, or even a lose-lose one. More importantly, you have not made a bad situation worse.

Julie

Julie was tired of the constant bickering in her marriage and her husband's frequent absences with his busy medical practice and recreational pursuits. After over twenty years of neglect she determined to leave him. Though she was convinced she was making the right decision, it was difficult for her to actually take the steps to go through with the divorce. When the initial phase was over and she and her husband were unable to come to a quick resolution of the property division and alimony, she went into severe depression. The divorce was put on hold for six months while she went into residential treatment. She could not face the failure of her life. She could not face her grown children who were convinced she was making a mistake. She could not face the consequence of her decisions and found no joy in her life. Ultimately, after several months, she became competent enough to begin meeting with her attorney again and finally reached a settlement with her husband on the terms of the divorce. However, the process left her angry and bitter about the stinginess of her husband. She compromised considerably because she did not want to go through a trial. It will be a long time before she feels any reason to be happy again.

Jack

Jack had a beautiful wife and three lovely children. Jack worked hard and knew how to invest money. Unfortunately, he did not do so well with the day-to-day management of his assets. His house was mortgaged to the hilt.

Jack's children loved him but were afraid to make him angry since he had occasionally erupted and would follow the kids around with a stick, swatting their legs to hurry them up in completing their chores. When Jack's 14-year-old son went to school with a black eye and told the school counselor he would not return home, the Division of Family Services began investigating. They ultimately obtained a Protective Order for the children and had Jack removed from the home. While he was out of the house, his wife obtained a Protective Order for herself as well and also filed for divorce.

Jack could not believe that his wife really wanted to leave him. It was inconceivable. They had always declared that they would stay together forever. Yes, they had problems, but that was because everyone did not see things the same way he did. In his mind, there was no reason for a divorce.

Jack's therapist prescribed antidepressants, but taking the pills did not make his wife return. Jack tried talking to her in the hall at court and was charged with violating the protective order. Jack's wife and his children were all in counseling and his attorney told him she was not coming back. The children that would visit him could only do so under supervision. For months Jack dragged out the legal proceedings in hopes of reconciliation. When Jack finally admitted to himself that he really had lost control over his wife and his family, he went to bed one night with a bottle of pills and did not wake up.

Studies have shown that 60% of divorces have medium to high levels of conflict. That is a lot of pain for everyone involved, including children, extended family, and mutual friends. To the extent the attitudes of selfishness and greed exist in your marriage, they will affect how a spouse acts throughout the divorce process. There are a number of divorces where one or both people involved are simply too angry, shocked, bitter, stubborn, or "crazy" to negotiate the terms of a divorce. They are just not there yet. For these individuals, court may be the only option; however, the system will not make them less angry.

Divorce represents too great a trauma for most people, including those who pretend they are handling it just fine. To the extent individuals are incapacitated emotionally, they are unable to assist in negotiating the terms of their divorce. Therefore, I frequently recommend some type of therapeutic intervention for my clients. A good attorney should recognize this dilemma and work with it, when necessary.

Overcoming the pain of a divorce will be a lengthy process, sometimes lasting years. I always advise my clients to wait at least two years before considering remarriage since it usually takes at least that long to process the emotional upheaval through which they have passed. On more than one occasion, those clients who have ignored this advice have been back in my office within a year or two for a subsequent divorce. If you happen to be the kind of person who keeps picking losers, remember the "old country" matchmaker. At least seek a trusted family member or friend's advice the next time around. The grass is not always greener with someone else. There is little comfort in the knowledge that second marriages have a higher divorce rate than first ones.

Whatever the level of conflict leading to your divorce, there will be emotional fallout to some degree. If you are a person who believes you can pretend your personal pain does not exist or it does not matter, think again.

PERSONAL PAIN DOES NOT STAY HOME

Divorce Negatively Impacts Your Employment

DIVORCE IS PERSONAL

LOSE FOCUS; REDUCE PRODUCTIVITY

ALL PARENTS GO TO WORK

STRAIN THE FAMILY BUSINESS

While we all pay lip service to the concept that you should not bring your personal problems to work, there are few individuals who can avoid it when going through a divorce. Attorneys joke that any spouse facing the prospect of paying alimony automatically begins to make less money, but there may be some truth to the phenomenon. It is not uncommon for individuals to lose their job while going through a divorce. Reduced productivity is almost a given. The stress of a divorce impacts some people more than others, of course, but most people cannot help being affected at work. They talk about it, think about it, brood about it, and take time off from work to deal with it. Court hearings, meetings with lawyers, and therapy for the kids all take a toll. You may be dealing with grief, loss, shock or any number of emotions that reduce your ability to concentrate and focus on your job. If you are fortunate, you will have a compassionate boss or partner who is willing to hold down the fort for a while, but typically patience will wear thin sooner or later.

Not infrequently, you may be involved in a business with your spouse, or worse, his or her family. Then you have not only all the anticipated problems with your job, but have to include division of the business as part of the divorce process itself. One of you may have to buy out the other, which can become a financial hardship on many small businesses. The partner who is leaving is blamed for destroying the family business as well as the family. The complications increase exponentially.

If you have been a stay-at-home parent caring for your children, it's likely you will not be able to continue in that role. The law presumes, and in most states requires, that both parents financially support their children. That means even if you are not employed, the court must calculate child support and/or alimony as if you were and at whatever rate of income you are most qualified to make. The practical effect of this is both parents will need to work. For someone who has not been in the work force for several years, this is another adjustment. Learning how to do a new job is usually a stressful event for most people. This stress will be in addition to dealing with all the other emotional and financial issues created by a divorce.

What about the spouse who has spent ten years supporting the other spouse through some type of professional school or vocational training? The spouse with the training and/or degree is now in a position to work at employment that is lucrative and rewarding while the other spouse may have ten years of experience in clerical or menial work, as well as parenting. The goal of rehabilitative alimony is to allow that spouse the opportunity for more education or training in order to be viable in the work force. However, frequently in the real world the alimony is not forthcoming or comes irregularly. Therefore, it cannot always be counted on for that assistance. In those cases, the spouse who needs the training often does not get it; he or she continues to work at the dead end job, living from paycheck to paycheck.

Then there is the spouse who worked for years for free to help the other spouse get their business off the ground. It could be anything from a jewelry store to a dental practice. If the jeweler wants to leave the marriage with the store, the other spouse is left with no ability to maintain that type of income, even if he or she receives a settlement for a portion of the business. If the spouse who has been keeping the books leaves, the dentist or jeweler or contractor has to figure out how to manage the finances, find a way to buy out that spouse, and still keep the business viable. Some types of businesses are more susceptible to this dilemma than others.

Many people are not aware that health insurance companies offering policies for coverage to employees cannot continue to insure a divorced spouse of the employee. The children may remain on the policy, but the divorced spouse has to obtain his or her own coverage, either through their own employer, if available, or through COBRA. COBRA is an acronym for a federal law[3], which requires insurance companies to make health insurance coverage available in these circumstances. However, the coverage is only for a limited time, typically 18 months to three years, and it is fairly expensive. In calculating your new post-divorce budget, you will need to determine if this extra expense is something you are going to require.

Linda finally found the courage to file for divorce after her husband came home drunk and beat her because she had the nerve to show up at the bar where he was hanging out with his girlfriend and his buddies. The problem was Linda had no job skills and worked as a teacher's aide in the local school district at a minimal wage. The job was paid by the hour and there was no way she could keep taking time off for court hearings, mandated mediation, and meetings with her attorney.

[3] COBRA stands for Consolidated Omnibus Budget Reconciliation Act.

Fortunately, Linda's boss was understanding about her many absences, but her boss did not have the authority to get her paid when she was not there. Because she was not a permanent employee Linda had no benefits or sick leave. While it seemed no one in the judicial system understood that if she did not work she did not get paid, her lawyer explained it is simply unworkable for the court to try to calendar hearings around everyone's work schedule. Nevertheless, she desperately needed the money to pay her bills, particularly when the temporary alimony did not arrive on time, which happened frequently.

After the divorce Linda's husband just simply refused to abide by the terms of the decree. He filed motion after motion to try and get the divorce set aside, to get the stipulation revoked, and finally to modify the divorce decree. When Linda refused to negotiate a revised order, her ex-husband hauled her back into court again. Linda had won all the other motions and the court had awarded her judgment for her attorneys' fees; however, her ex-husband was not paying the judgments. The state would garnish his wages for child support and alimony, but not for attorneys' fees judgments.

Meanwhile, Linda was feeling very ill. She was always tired and had no energy. At first, she had no insurance after the divorce because her ex-husband's policy could not cover her. Eventually she was able to increase her hours to full time and obtain health coverage before she went into the doctor and was ultimately diagnosed with a life-threatening illness. However, trying to balance court appearances with medical treatments and still keep up appearances at her job was almost more than she could manage. Ultimately, her ex-husband had to convey ownership to her of some real property he owned in order to satisfy all the judgments against him. Two years after litigation started, the divorce and post-divorce fight was finally over. Fortunately, Linda managed to hang on to her job while she completed her treatments and began to rebuild her life.

Rick

Rick was working at the local steel mill when his wife told him she was leaving him. While he knew it was coming, he still hoped she would reconsider. When it was clear that was not going to happen he hired an attorney and began going through the process of obtaining temporary orders. There were many debts and not enough money to go around. While the court appeared somewhat sympathetic to that problem, the judge told him he was to do his best. He was expected to pay the bills, child support, and alimony and still have a place to live.

Work began to slide down on Rick's list of priorities. The days were long and boring and the nights were lonely and even longer. Occasionally he fell asleep at work. Once he got caught and was written up for the infraction. He began using marijuana again, just enough to take off the edge and make life bearable.

Business was not good at the steel plant. The owners kept trying to refinance their debt in order to stay in business. There were always layoffs. In fact, Rick was laid off before the divorce was over. So he asked the court to reduce his financial obligations. The judge, however, was convinced he would soon be back to work and refused to lower support.

After the divorce, Rick did get called back to work. By then, he was fighting depression and using marijuana more and more frequently. Within a year of the divorce, he got caught again on a random drug test at work and was fired.

If you intend to seek a divorce or find yourself involuntarily involved in one, the best you can do is to let your supervisors know your situation and try to be sensitive to their needs. Your employment is critical at this time, not only for the income needed for support, but also for the stability and insurance benefits it provides. Find ways to make it up to your employer when you have to be gone. Do what you can to be aware of the potential problems here and stay focused as much as you can. Some people actually find work to be an escape from the pain of the divorce process, at least for a time.

Whatever the situation at work, the series of problems can often eventually lead to a negative impact on available income. This means a reduced ability to support the family at a time when expenses are increasing. That dilemma adds to the already increased stress, which perpetuates the problems at work, and the cycle continues. If you believe you can go through a divorce and really keep all your personal problems at home, think again.

5

"IS IT MY FAULT?"

*Divorce Traumatizes
Your Children*

CHILDREN'S ATTITUDES MIRROR THEIR PARENTS' ATTITUDE

MAJORITY OF DIVORCES INVOLVE CONFLICT

DIVORCE "SUCKS" FROM CHILD'S POINT OF VIEW

CHILDREN LEARN TO EXPLOIT PARENTAL CONFLICT

Volumes are written on how divorce affects children and how children can recover from their parents' divorce. Some experts claim children are shattered by family break up while others opine they deal with it well as a growing experience. No matter what you believe about this issue, there are some constants I have observed.

In a typical divorce, whatever that is, psychologists report children do best when they have maximum exposure to both parents. However, this does not necessarily mean equal time with each parent, since studies also show that as children get older they often need a home base. Frequently, parents who divide their children 50/50 are servicing the divorcing parents, not the children. Often children will deal with the divorce as they see their parents deal with it. They are, after all, your children. However, at times children may wear a mask to hide their true feelings in order to please their parents or keep the peace.

People who are truly able to put their children's best interests ahead of their own grief or pain generally come up with a parenting plan which allows access by both parents, with a certain amount of structure. They consult with each other regarding issues of health, education, and the general welfare of the children. Being a teenager in this country is a challenge that few children come through unscathed. If parents cooperate with each other in administering discipline and inevitable disputes with their children, there is a better chance the children will survive adolescence without any permanent damage. However, statistics show this is the minority of cases, as medium to high conflict occurs more often. Remember, it only takes one parent to create conflict and inflict the subsequent damage on their children.

Of course, no parent admits they are hurting their children. The pain is always part of a process to protect the child, or teach their ex-spouse a lesson so he/she will not take advantage of them again. Parents claim that what they are doing is for the "best interests" of the children. Like the crusades, or the inquisition, unspeakable horrors are justified in the name of religion, or in divorce litigation, the best interests of the child. Obviously, the claim alone does not make it valid.

If a parent would look at a divorce from a child's point of view, they might slow down just a bit. Yet most parents going through a divorce are preoccupied with their own pain and often do not realize the additional pain they inflict on their children. For children who have been living in a house with physical or verbal conflict, a divorce may actually be a way to peace. Even then, however, the conflict does not end, it just moves into a different arena.

For the majority of children, a divorce means the end of the only way of life they have known. Their parent moved out of the house. They now will see that parent on a schedule, created for them to meet the needs of the parents. From now on the children will move back and forth, from Dad's house to Mom's house, at least once every week or two. This is a lot of packing and unpacking of that overnight bag. If Mom was a stay-at-home mom before, she will not be now. In that case, this means some children have essentially lost two parents, not just one. Dad may not be around when they need his help with history, though he was the one who "knew all that stuff", and Mom may not be available when they fall down and get hurt or "just want Mom". From now on any social event or activity in which they are participating or being honored is going to be awkward because both Mom and Dad want to come but do not want to speak to one another. High school graduations, weddings, funerals, recitals, Halloween, and visits with grandchildren all have to be split or shared. And this is the best-case scenario.

What about the children whose parents now have different values, rules, morals and schedules? It is very common for at least one divorcing spouse to have a dramatic change in values after a divorce. No one figures out faster than teenagers when Dad is mad at Mom because she let them do something he thinks they should not have been allowed to do. No one knows better than teenagers of divorced parents that if they can keep their parents fighting and off balance enough, the parents will be so distracted that the kids will be forgotten and can do pretty much what they want.

This can be a complicated issue. While most parents would agree their kids should not be taking drugs, for example, they frequently disagree on many other activities, which may or may not lead a child to that course. How do you feel about rated "R" movies, tank tops, thong underwear, church on Sunday, tattoos, body piercing, and pre-marital sex? Is Boy Scouts or sports a big part of your child's life that you want to encourage, or is it an extra you cannot afford and will not bother with right now? Is Aunt Brook's wedding a justifiable excuse to alter the visitation or parenting schedule or will only a death in the family qualify? If Dad had Christmas last year but missed his summer vacation with the children because of circumstances beyond his control, should he get them for Christmas again this year? What about half of Christmas? If you cannot agree, then you can have a judge decide. But Christmas may be over with by the time you get into court, so your frustration levels rise and the kids are the closest ones to hear about it.

I have had parents tell me with a straight face they believe it is absolutely necessary for their children know that the other parent has lied to them about something. I know parents who leave home with the children when the other parent is ten minutes late for a scheduled pick up. There are parents who argue in the driveway while their children are in the car. Some parents tell their children five minutes before it is time to go home they should call the other parent and ask if they can stay longer, which is a set up for the other parent. Other parents tell their children they cannot afford to do anything or buy anything or go anywhere because the ex-spouse either "takes all my money" or "does not pay me what he is supposed to".

These are the more subtle tactics parents use. There are, of course, plenty of direct methods of attack as well, where children are literally pawns in the battle. Parents tell their children what a "slut" their mother is, or what a "deadbeat" they have for a father. One "loving" father drove his children to every site where he knew his ex-wife had slept with the man with whom she had an affair, since he thought they deserved to know the truth about their mother. A father who refused to participate in court-ordered family therapy told his children they did not need therapy since the only one who was crazy was their mother. That father convinced his teenager to report her mother to child protective services when the mother used a steak knife to unlock the teenager's door because her daughter had refused to come out and do her chores. The teenager jumped at her mother as she came in the room and got scratched in the process. Another mother would call the police every time she got into a verbal argument with father and another continually reinforced that the children needed to be afraid of their father since they never knew when he would "lose it". The parents' relationship deteriorates into a black game of getting even.

These scenarios do not include the thousands of cases where parents have physically or sexually abused their children and deserve limited access. Other than this last category, most parents carry out all these activities with a firm delusion, albeit sometimes thoughtlessly, that what they are doing is good for their children.

I do not know how many times and ways divorced parents can be told that any time they say something demeaning about their child's other parent, either directly or by inference, the people that they hurt the most are their own children. As I tried to explain to one mother who was convinced that her 16-year-old daughter would be much better off if her ex-husband disappeared from the planet, that 16-year-old is half Dad. When you tell her that her father is worthless, you tell her that half of her is worthless too.

The office of the Guardian Ad Litem[†] in my state has created a "Bill of Rights" for children whose parents are in conflict. This Bill of Rights states that children should be free to love both parents. This should apply no matter what their parents have done to each other. One 16-year-old boy of warring parents was so excited when I showed this to him that he asked for it in wallet size. Children should feel free to have their mother's picture by their bed when they are at their father's house and vice versa. They should be able to call either parent from the other parent's home, within reason.

However, calling a parent should not be a way to avoid discipline. Just as when they were married, parents

[†]*Guardian ad Litem is an attorney appointed to represent children, often in cases where abuse or neglect is alleged.*

should discuss discipline strategies and other issues regarding their children out of their children's presence. If parents do not present a united front, these children may, and frequently do, exploit the situation.

Children need and deserve to be raised by caring and loving parents who bring them light, guide them, and teach them how to be responsible adults. Few parents can do this while they are embroiled in litigation. Instead, children are "parentified" as they become their parents' confidante and comforter. Nothing is more painful for a child than to be forced to pick sides. Children quickly learn to tell the parent with whom they are spending time whatever they believe that parent wants to hear.

American Family Mediators conducted a study with adult children of divorce. The children they interviewed identified many instances in which they were the subject of ongoing litigation and custody disputes. Frequently the children were asked by one parent, "Where do you want to live?" Many parents believe it is appropriate to ask a child this question at the time of the divorce, or believe a child should choose his or her home of preference at a certain age. Many people are surprised to learn that usually nothing is more unfair to a child.

Consider this example: when a child is asked by her father, "Do you want to live with me?" she is placed in a no-win situation. If she says, "Yes", she immediately feels disloyal to her mother. If she says, "No" she fears she has hurt her father. Since she is with her father, chances are she will say, "Yes". However, this is not necessarily how she really feels. In fact, according to the study, this is exactly how it goes. Then when she says, "Yes", Father is thrilled and immediately says, "Are you sure?" to which she must respond, "Of course!" Father then proceeds to get an attorney and initiate custody litigation. Somewhere in the next year or two of emotional turmoil and conflict, a therapist will finally discover that the child is quite happy at Mother's home but enjoys very much being with Dad and does not want to lose the closeness of that relationship. Now Father is really frustrated and angry because he has spent thousands of dollars on litigation, daughter is embarrassed and confused, and Mother is hurt.

What if a child, particularly a teenager, really wants to live with Dad and says so? What the child does not say is the reason she wants to live with Dad is because Dad has fewer rules, Dad will let her go out later at night, and Dad does not hate her boyfriend nearly as much as Mom does.

Is it really in the daughter's best interests to live with her Dad? Should a teenager's desires control the outcome?

What about when Johnny is living with Dad and Mom inherits some money? Now Mom is saying to Johnny, "If you will come live with me, I will buy you a new car." Dad does not believe Johnny should have a car yet and cannot afford the insurance if he does get one. Is buying a teenager's custody acting in the best interest of that child? This happens all the time.

There are times when there are legitimate reasons to change custody. However, in my experience, most young children just want love and peace, and most teenagers just want to be left alone to hang out with their friends. They prefer living with the parent who will allow them to do that the most and with the least resistance. It seems obvious that a child's desires should not be the only criteria for selecting their home base residence, though courts will typically give that some weight. However, most therapists would agree children should never be asked directly where they want to live. Therapists may question a child about what they like at Mom's house or what's fun at Dad's and draw their own conclusions, making recommendations accordingly.

Tammy

Tammy divorced John five years ago but the conflict never ended. Their daughter Jessica had just turned 16 and was constantly fighting with her mother. Tammy liked to manage her home with a great deal of structure. It helped her manage the blended family she now had with her new husband and his three children. There were rules for homework, chores, curfew, church, and family activities. One night Jessica came home hours after curfew and the fallout was intense. Jessica was so angry that she ran away from home and eventually turned up at Dad's house.

John was re-married to Rhonda, who tolerated his impulsive lifestyle much better than Tammy. His home life was very different from Tammy's since there were no children there. He and Rhonda both worked and usually relaxed in the evenings with a few friends and beer to go around. John had been a relatively indifferent father to this point, though he did care for his children. Because he felt it was not worth fighting with Tammy about every other weekend, he often waived his right to spend time with the children, which suited Tammy just fine. His absence created less opportunity for him to be a "bad influence" on the children. Jessica decided life at Dad's was a lot more fun than life at home and begged her dad to let her stay for a while.

Tammy was furious when she discovered Jessica was "hiding out" at John's and insisted John send her home immediately. John asked Jessica if she was sure she wanted to stay at his place because, if she did, he'd "fight" for her. Two weeks into her new life Jessica was sure. John hired a lawyer and filed suit for custody.

By the time the case came to court, Jessica and Dad had already become tired of each other. They fought almost as much as Mom and Jessica, only about different things. At the courthouse, the attorneys were trying to find a compromise that would satisfy everyone. They finally agreed to let Jessica speak to the judge alone and tell him what she really wanted, since both parents claimed she had said she wanted to live with them. The judge met with the attorneys afterwards and announced, "Jessica does not really care who she lives with so long as she can be with her friends."

Jessica went back to live with her mother who continued to fight with her father. She ran away several more times. The last time she came home she was 17 and pregnant.

Joel

Joel and Felicia had two teenage boys when Felicia decided to leave. She took the boys with her and moved across country to get as far away from Joel as possible. Angry and bitter, she refused to even ask for alimony or part of Joel's retirement in spite of her attorney's advice. She had made a new start in a new place and wanted to completely forget about Joel's existence.

Unfortunately, Felicia's sons did not feel the same way about their father. Initially, they spoke with him very little since Mom had convinced them he was the source of their problems and the reason they had to move so far away. When they did talk to him Mom got upset so it was easier to leave things alone. However, as the months went by, Dad would continue to call and offer whatever encouragement, advice, or news they would accept. Eventually, they were calling him on a regular basis to talk about football, school and girls.

Felicia became angry whenever she found out they were talking to Joel. She fought with the boys about it. She insisted they could not be friends with this man if they loved her. As soon as the oldest son, Jonathan, graduated from high school, he left and went to live with his dad. After six months of silence, Felicia finally began accepting phone calls from Jonathan, but she was still resentful. The next summer the youngest son, Kelly, now 16, became angry with his mother because of her refusal to allow him to have a relationship with his father. They fought about other things as well. Kelly quit going to school and eventually was kicked off the football team, the only thing he enjoyed. He became belligerent and Felicia threw him out of the house. Kelly went to live with his buddy.

Jonathan flew home to assess the situation and talk to Kelly; he told Dad to do whatever was necessary to get Kelly out of Mom's custody. Joel flew out and tried to negotiate with Felicia, but she refused to talk to him because she was convinced he had orchestrated the scenario to deprive her of her children, and refused to talk to him. While the attorneys were trying to resolve the issue, Kelly went back to Mom's house to insist she sign the papers to transfer custody to his father. Felicia refused to open the door and Kelly knocked it down. Felicia claimed she was afraid and called the police who promptly arrested Kelly and landed him in juvenile detention.

Eventually the lawyers got Kelly released from detention, custody was transferred to Joel and everyone was in counseling except Felicia, who refused to participate. The result is a very angry and confused 16-year-old boy who still does not understand why he is in so much pain.

The only time children will not become victims of your divorce is if you, as a parent, can learn to take the high road in your interaction with your former spouse. You need to learn to communicate with your co-parent. If you never get this far, your children will suffer. Hopefully, you can graduate from communication to cooperation, and maybe progress through forgiveness to actually reach compassion. By being compassionate to your children's other parent, the children will recognize more clearly than anything else you could do that the problems that caused the divorce were not their fault. No matter what you tell children, many of them still believe that if they had behaved themselves, done their chores, been a good girl, done their homework, earned better grades, or gotten along better with their brothers and sisters, the divorce would not have happened. When parents use their children as the basis for continuing conflict, it reinforces the children's perception that it was their fault. There's nothing you can say to convince them otherwise.

One of my favorite books, entitled **Dear Judge, Kid's Letters to the Judge**, is a collection of letters written by children of divorce to the person they perceive as having ultimate power in their situation. The classic example was the child who wrote to the judge and told him that he should "undo" his parents' divorce because it was just "not working out". If you believe you can remove one parent from your child's life without some type of traumatic effect on that child now or much later, think again.

6

THE MYTH OF BEING FREE

Divorce Complicates Your Life

**DIVORCE RARELY REMOVES YOUR
SPOUSE FROM YOUR LIFE**

CHILDREN CONNECT YOU TO YOUR SPOUSE FOREVER

DATING WITH BAGGAGE IS TRICKY

**SECOND FAMILIES, STEP FAMILIES,
BLENDED FAMILIES ARE PROBLEMATIC**

Most people get divorced because they believe it will make their life better. There is a perception that if you can get rid of the "jerk", or the "witch", things will go more smoothly. However, getting rid of the other spouse is a virtual impossibility if you have children. Children will keep you connected to their other parent at least until the children are 18, and usually for long afterwards. All those weddings, graduations, grandchildren and special events in which children want their parents' participation do not disappear because your marriage dissolves. At a minimum, if both parents live in the same area, there will be a weekly or biweekly transfer of children and other related contact. That is not counting attendance at special activities at school, recitals, sporting events, parent teacher conference, Boy Scout banquets, and so on and so on. While people divorce each other, they do not divorce their children, though one child did file for a divorce from her parents in Florida.

While you no longer live with this person after divorce, you are still connected. Usually your life will become *more* complicated, not less, after a divorce. So long as you stay single, you have all the responsibility of a single parent. If you are the custodial parent, you are playing the role of provider and nurturer for your children, though you hopefully will have some assistance. You will work all day and care for children and your home at night. You may have day care costs you did not have before, and you may or may not have success receiving the child support from your other parent.

If you are a non-custodial parent, you may find yourself constantly trying to find out what is going on with the children's activities. When is that soccer game? Your son cannot remember and the schedule is on the fridge at Mom's house. You want to have normal parenting time but the kids only visit for the weekend. What if you have an argument with your teenage daughter and she leaves in a huff? She can avoid you indefinitely now that she does not live with you anymore.

Statistics show that both you and your spouse are very likely to remarry. Before you arrive at that point, however, you have to get back into the dating game. Only this time, you have the extra baggage of an ex-spouse and children. Most likely the people you will be dating have the same extra baggage. You are dating around work schedules, parenting schedules, and children's schedules. Not only do you have to try and please your new boyfriend or girl-friend, you probably have to try and garner the approval of the children. If that is not complicated enough, you throw a new spouse into the mix.

While 50 percent of first marriages end in divorce, the divorce statistics for remarriages that end in divorce are 60 percent. There are a lot of reasons for this. After you have gone through the trauma of divorce once, it is a more acceptable alternative the second time around (or for some, the third, fourth, and even fifth time around). In addition to familiarity with the process, the stress on a relationship in a second or subsequent marriage frequently leads to a subsequent divorce. After remarriage, your life is now complicated by a new spouse and maybe step children, along with their extended families and their ex-spouses, together with all the emotional entanglements and interaction that entails. And remember, it is not only your relationship with all these people that will be a factor in your new family dynamics. You also have to deal with the relationship of your children to their new stepparent, your step children's relationship with your own children, your relationship with your new spouse's ex-spouse, and possibly the ex-spouse's new spouse, and eventually, your ex-spouse's new spouse and their children, together with those children's relationship with your children. It truly can become a dizzying prospect. Just keeping the schedule straight for all the comings and goings is a Herculean task, never mind making sure people actually get along. If any one of these people chooses to be unreasonable around parenting issues, money, or any one of innumerable topics, life quickly becomes overwhelming. It is not uncommon or even particularly difficult for your children, the children of your new spouse, or your ex-spouse's new spouse to sabotage a marriage.

Then there is the financial side of subsequent marriages. Is it her money, his money, their money, or the children's money? Was his house now their house, or still his house? What did she bring into the marriage and what can she take away from it if it does not last? Should he keep his money separate or be "committed" to the new marriage by pooling their resources to make a new family?

Jenny entered her third marriage with a commitment to make it work. She fully intended to make her house a home for her children and Sam's children. She spent a great deal of money, which she had inherited just prior to her marriage, to set up house. During the marriage she worked part time, but spent most of her time taking care of kids and home. Jenny inherited more money about a year into the marriage. Together with money from property Sam owned before they got married, they purchased a lot and began building their dream house. Sam had some skill in construction and did a lot of the work himself.

In spite of her good intentions, there was conflict almost from the beginning. Sam was not the same guy after they got married; no matter what she did, it was not right. He yelled and cursed, and told her she spent too much money. Jenny was devastated to discover Sam did not appreciate her sacrifices or understand her feelings and the pressure she was under. Her first husband was filing petitions against her, pursuing custody of her children, supported by claims made in nasty affidavits from husband number two. That court case took a great deal of emotion and cash to defend. Jenny's children watched the fighting and frequently became a target for Sam's anger as well.

Sam was convinced that Jenny was frivolous and incapable of managing her money. He spent much time entertaining his children from his first marriage. They were first in his life and when they were at the house, Jenny and her children took a back seat. Frequently, Jenny's children were not invited when Sam went boating or skiing with his children. Hurt feelings grew to deeper anger and resentment.

Sam and Jenny separated and reconciled, then separated again. Meanwhile, they kept working on the house. The children all helped to some extent. After two years, Sam decided he had had enough and filed for divorce. Jenny was crushed. They could not agree on anything. Counting the money she had inherited just before the marriage, Jenny discovered she had gone through about $130,000. It was all gone. Sam had sold the house he owned before the marriage and refinanced another property. The cash from those transactions was all gone as well. Everything went into living expenses and building the house. Sam claimed his money had gone into building the house and Jenny's money had gone to living expenses and trivial spending. Jenny felt that Sam had connived her into spending all her inheritance, leaving her with nothing. A court battle began that lasted two years. Though the attorneys' fees cost over $25,000, Jenny had little choice but to go to court since Sam refused to offer her anything. Eventually Jenny was awarded $40,000 from Sam for her share of the equity in the house. Sam was awarded the house, but had to sell it to pay Jenny and his own attorneys' fees. The children left their former family with a mutual hatred for their stepparent and stepsiblings.

Brent

Brent and Kelly had been married for fifteen years and had five children at the time they finally decided to call it quits. Though Brent was actually the one who left the marriage, he was a little taken back when Kelly remarried relatively quickly. She married Kyle, who had custody of his two teenage sons. These boys had plenty of emotional baggage of their own since their mother had abandoned them for a lifestyle of drugs and parties. The boys, added to Kelly's five children, created a large houseful.

Eventually Brent met someone and also remarried. Trish had three little girls with an enormous amount of energy. When Brent's children came to spend weekends with their dad, Brent often left the little girls with his oldest child, Todd, age 16. Todd resented it since Dad "never really asked." Besides, he came over to see his Dad, "not to be a babysitter".

Brent's 14-year-old daughter, Jenny, did not get along with Brent's new wife. She resented the time Trish took away from her relationship with her Dad, which had already been severely limited because of the divorce. Jenny knew Trish was trying to buy the affection of her brothers and sisters, but she was not interested.

Meanwhile, Brent and Trish started having trouble, and Trish and the girls moved out for a temporary separation. One weekend a few weeks later, Brent had managed to talk Trish into spending the day with him. He dropped the three girls off in Todd's bedroom, since he was there for the weekend anyway, and spent the morning with Trish. Trish actually agreed to come back that night for dinner and he had his hands full trying to juggle those plans with the fact that his children were there for the weekend as well. About the time Trish was supposed to show up, Todd and Dad got into an argument. Todd told his dad he was leaving and started walking. Brent was torn between following Todd and preparing for Trish's imminent arrival. He opted for saving his marriage. Todd was amazed when Dad did not come after him and actually allowed him to walk home five miles. He did not speak to his father for months.

Ecclesiastical leaders have told me that many people who are entangled in subsequent marriages, blended families, and associated conflict, come to them for counsel. Frequently, these individuals admit they wish they had not sought a divorce in the first place, but had instead spent the energy repairing the original marriage. As one three-time divorcee observed, "You never know what baggage a new spouse brings to the marriage until they move in and unpack." Some people do find a new spouse that is a better fit for them, and they are happy. However, many people learn the hard way that often the problems that lead to a divorce are still with them. It is not a new partner they need, but better skills in communicating, negotiating, and problem solving. If you believe your life will be easier and simpler after divorce or with a different partner, think again.

7

WHERE DID ALL THE PARENTS GO?

Divorce Damages Society

UNRESOLVED CONFLICT CYCLES
TO NEXT GENERATION

PARENTS IN CRISIS DO NOT VOLUNTEER

SPIRITUAL DEATH TURNS PEOPLE NUMB

SELFISH-BASED DECISIONS
DESTROY COMMUNITY

I am aware that some believe it is old fashioned, but I truly believe, deep down, that families are still the most viable core unit for our society. Children need and deserve a home with parents who love them, nurture them, and teach them how to be responsible adults. Without this foundation, children grow up, but they are not "raised".

When families are in conflict, there are many repercussions for society as a whole, as well as the individuals in the family. The children are the obvious losers. They do not receive the emotional support and nurturing they need when their family's energy is expended in conflict. Much of the family resources may be spent on litigation, experts, mediators, special masters, and therapy, all in an effort to make things right again. This obviously translates into less resources for raising children in a meaningful way. Those things that can be lost include computers, school supplies, field trips, outings for special occasions, and family vacations. We are in an age where a child, practically speaking, needs a computer and Internet access to keep up in school. To get ahead, they need the opportunities of special programs, extra-curricular activities, and varied experiences. When family time, energy, and resources are used up in going through a divorce and dealing with the aftermath, those opportunities may pass them by.

If children are not getting ahead or even keeping up, they fall behind academically, socially, and emotionally. They become fearful, self-absorbed adults who are incapable of caring for themselves, let alone creating a healthy family of their own. They create walls to protect themselves from the pain which surrounds them and, frequently, they are unaware of and out of touch with their feelings. Unprepared for the world of mature relationships, they repeat the only script of which they are aware. The conflict goes on to the next generation, where the cycle continues and spreads. Statistically, children of divorce are more likely to go through a divorce themselves. In this case, the "sins of the fathers" do visit the next generations and often succeeding generations as well.

Society is also affected by the post-divorce demands on parents. The law presumes that every parent is employed. Frequently, both parents are employed in two parent homes, but, in that situation, they can help and support each other to meet the needs of the family unit. After a divorce, both parents are now working to support their separate respective homes and then they have to take care of those homes and the needs of the children alone. If they remarry, they frequently have to deal with the time consuming and energy draining issues of new children, step-children, and blended families. These parents are tired, with good reason, and, frequently, in crisis. Rarely do they have the energy or time to provide any of the volunteer work and service that helps fill in the gaps in the neighborhood. The story-time lady at the library, the parent aide at school, and the volunteer in the high school shop class are often roles filled by parents with the energy, resources, or ability to donate that time or expertise. The community loses the resources of those individuals who might have donated their services but no longer have the time or energy to do it.

One of the most significant consequences of divorce that I see is what I call a spiritual death for many individuals. The pain that leads to the divorce and perpetuates through the divorce process is so acute and traumatizing that people turn inward to protect themselves from further pain. They surround themselves with a cloak of numbness and, consequently, they deal with others at arms length. Hearts turn cold. There is a loss of charity and compassion. These attributes are vital to keeping a society connected.

Candace

Candace and Robert were both very attractive people who had a beautiful three-year-old daughter, Cory. Though divorced, they continued to fight frequently, making horrible accusations about each other. Robert's father, also divorced, supported Robert in his fight against Candace, making sure "that woman" did not get away with anything. Candace had been drinking again and was arrested for drunk driving. This time Cory was in the car. The arresting officers contacted Robert, who immediately picked up the child.

Robert and his father were both outraged at the mother's behavior and insisted that an immediate "ex parte"[5] custody order should be obtained to protect the child. A call to the sheriff's office to investigate these claims revealed that Candace had been intoxicated; however, the deputy reported that Robert appeared to have been drinking as well, when he picked up the child. She had reluctantly turned the child over to Robert, only as the lesser of two evils. Further checking showed that Candace had previously obtained a protective order against Robert in another county for allegedly abusing her.

---

[5]The words "ex parte" mean that the order is obtained without providing advance notice to the other side. It is only available for extreme circumstances and effective for a limited time until a hearing is held within a specified number of days.

Robert, vigorously supported by Dad, was adamant that Candace was a danger to the child and immediate action was necessary. Robert's father hastened to explain that his ex-wife had constantly made up fictitious accounts of abuse to keep him from his children and he was not about to let that happen to his son. Now that all his children were over age 18 he could see them, but she had ruined their chances for a normal family.

The rage exhibited by both these men was only equaled by the anger of the child's mother when she sobered up and found out Robert had her child. The legal wrangling went on for years, interspersed with months of calm when Robert and Candace actually reconciled and moved in with each other periodically. If Robert ever tired of the litigation, his Dad would re-invigorate him for the fight. Candace's mother, also divorced, helped support her side of the war.

Robert and Candace actually loved each other quite passionately, but could not figure out how to constructively communicate when they disagreed about something. Married or divorced, they fought bitterly and constantly. Their parents did it, they do it, and it is unlikely that Cory will know how to do anything else.

Kyle

Deborah filed for divorce from Kyle because they fought about their adult children from previous marriages. This made three strikes for Kyle in the marriage arena. He was not surprised at the divorce complaint but felt he had something coming since he had worked on Deborah's house and cabin, helping with repairs and some remodeling. Things were more complicated because these two also were partners in a business. Several sales commissions were still outstanding and they could not agree on how the proceeds should be split between them. Meanwhile, the commissions were being held in escrow until they settled or a court could decide.

Deborah was angry that Kyle thought he was entitled to any interest in the house she owned before they were married. She had supported him during the marriage while most of his money went to pay support for other children and ex-wives. He was a "gold-digger" from the beginning, as far as she was concerned. She admitted he had helped replace a furnace once and did a little painting, but he lived in the house for a couple of years and should have been willing to help out without being paid for his labor.

It seemed like all of Kyle's income went to alimony and personal living expenses. He had given up church long ago. He was not involved in any school or community organizations. Divorce or not, he was determined to go on the cruise he had booked months before and could not figure out why Deborah was upset when he decided to go with someone else. After all, she had kicked him out.

Kyle was completely self-absorbed. If something made his life easier or more comfortable it was automatically desirable; conversely, if something was inconvenient, required effort, or was unlikely to bring him a direct benefit, it was of no value and therefore was discarded or ignored. Once Deborah decided to end the marriage, Kyle was ready to move on, since it was too much hassle to live with her anymore anyway.

At some point, we, as a people, need to look at the whole picture of our lives. We should come to a point where we ask ourselves, "What is the purpose of my life or anyone's life?" Ultimately, each of us has to decide if we believe we are here to take whatever we can from our time on this planet, or if we are here to serve and help each other make the world a better place. Divorce has a way of convincing many that the former philosophy is preferable to the latter. When people no longer care for each other and make all decisions based only upon their own self-interest, eventually the community will fall from its own weight. No one will care about the community as a whole, and, if no one cares, no one will assist in maintaining it. The logical end of that cycle will be chaos and anarchy.

Our society is fast moving and filled with special effects. We e-mail our family and friends and look for the latest gadgets to make our lives more convenient. As therapists and spiritualists report that personal relationships are the most significant factor in meeting our desires for fulfillment, our culture races away from a lifestyle that encourages that type of interaction. Everyone is in a hurry. They are too busy and too tired. It is so much easier to avoid interpersonal relations than to "try and figure out what that woman wants", or to "try talking to that impossible man". However, unless you are resigned to dying alone, unmissed and unloved, you will need to learn to effectively communicate with those closest to you. Why not learn it now, with this spouse, and save a family? Our community is made up of families in a variety of homes, and if you think your divorce will not distress and diminish your community, think again.

DECISION TIME

While many couples think getting out of a relationship will solve their problems, therapists point out that if you do not deal with the issues that damaged this relationship, it is likely those issues will continue to impact future relationships as well. This is not rocket science, but few of us seem to get it. Divorce and remarriage without an identification, examination and resolution of the problems leading to the divorce is like changing gloves without washing your hands.

Studies now verify the notion that divorce makes unhappily married adults happier is a myth. According to researchers at the University of Chicago, unhappily married adults who divorced were no happier five years after the divorce than equally unhappy married adults who remained together.

In a study by the Institute for American Values, two-thirds of unhappily married people who remained married reported that their marriages were happy five years later. In fact, 80 percent of those who rated their marriages as "very unhappy" said they were happily married five years later. The most startling statistic in this study shows that if a couple is unhappy, the chances of their being happy five years later is 64 percent if they remain together but only 19 percent if they divorce and remarry someone else.

These studies revealed three principle techniques used by those who choose to stay married. The first was endurance. Interviews established that some of those who found happiness eventually discovered that the sources of conflict, such as money, depression, and even infidelity eased with time. Other couples aggressively tackled their problems. They sought more private time, obtained counseling, or relied on family support. Finally, there were the "personal happiness seekers". These people found ways to improve their overall contentment in spite of their mediocre marriage.

A significant finding is the discovery of the impact of attitude toward marriage. Those who enter marriage with a dim view of divorce and a strong motivation for avoiding it are not only less likely to divorce, but less likely to be unhappy. As Sheryl Crow sings, "It's not having what you want; it's wanting what you've got."[6] Behavior follows attitude.

If you want to stay married, do not give up. In this information age, there are books, seminars, web pages, and innumerable other resources available to assist you in

[6]*"Soak Up the Sun"* by Sheryl Crow/Jeff Trott.

improving your marriage and in finding happiness, or at least contentment. It is true that sometimes the decision to divorce is taken from you by circumstances you cannot control. But for most people, it is not too late to save your marriage. It takes commitment, effort, and, for some, re-prioritizing.

I firmly believe that most people can stay married and be happy. Both partners should commit to find a way to make the marriage work instead of waiting for it to get better, waiting to fall back in love with their spouse, or waiting for their spouse to "wake up" and appreciate them. Get outside yourself and see what you can do to make the relationship better without relying on your spouse to fix it. As they say, "love is a verb," meaning it is something you do, not just something you say.

Another lawyer anecdote is the story of the woman who sought an attorney to help her divorce her husband. She informed the attorney she wanted to really hurt her spouse. The attorney looked her straight in the eye and advised her, "If you want to cause him the maximum pain, go home and be as nice, as sweet, and as kind as you know how to be. Serve him at every opportunity, and then, after six months, inform him you are leaving." The woman went home with great anticipation and immediately began carrying out the lawyer's instructions. Of course, as with most decent human beings, this woman's husband reciprocated her actions and, after six months, she no longer wanted a divorce because she had found her way to happiness. While the story may be simplistic, sometimes we make life more complicated than it needs to be. Frequently, happiness is a by-product of our endeavors, not the end result.

Certainly there are marriages that are impossible to save and divorced couples who are happier than if they had stayed married. There are abusers and control freaks and narcissists who will not be happy with anyone and with whom life can never be content. But for the rest of us, the benefits of divorce are overrated. Divorce sets into motion events over which you have little control, including the reaction of spouses and children, and the uncertainty of new relationships.

Divorce may be appropriate and necessary for you, but calculate the cost carefully. When you make the decision, weigh the risks for you, your spouse, and your children. Consider the impact on your extended family and that of your spouse. Recognize the financial drain and reduction of resources that will result. Realize that you will experience some level of personal loss, no matter how amicable the divorce. Your employment could be affected. Your children may be traumatized. In many ways, life will be more complicated than ever before as you strive to meet schedules often dictated by others. Most importantly, though the divorce may resolve some problems, others will arise. Will those problems be preferable to the ones you have now?

> *At the end of the generation, after the wounds are inflicted on your children, your family, and your community, will it have been worth it? If you are still sure, then you may be one of the few who should seek a divorce. But if you question it, if you hesitate, if you now think divorce could be a devastating upheaval that may not bring you the joy, peace, or relief that you are seeking, keep thinking.*

APPENDIX

1. *Family Matters*, published by Australian Institute of Family Studies, 300 Queen St., Melbourne, Victoria 3000, Australia, www.aifs.gov.au

2. *Does Divorce Make People Happy? Findings From a Study of Unhappy Marriages*, by Linda J. Waite, William J. Doherty, Maggie Gallagher, Ye Luo, and Scott M. Stanley. Sponsored by University of Chicago and Institute for American Values, 1841 Broadway Suite 211, New York, NY 10023, www.americanvalues.org.

3. *Cohabitation, Marriage, Divorce and Remarriage in the United States*, Report released 2002 by Center for Disease Control and Prevention, health statistics regarding marriage and divorce, www.cdc.gov.

4. *Guardian Ad Litem's office*, State of Utah, Utah County Children's Bill of Rights

5. *Dear Judge, Kid's Letters to the Judge*, Compiled by Charlotte Hardwick, Pale Horse Publishing, PO Box 1447 Livingston, Texas 77351-1447, 2002.

6. *Healing Hearts, Helping Children and Adults Recover From Divorce*, Elizabeth Hickey, MSW and Elizabeth Dalton, J.D., Gold Leaf Press, 2533 North Carson St., Suite 1544, Carson City, NV 89706, 1994.

7. *U.S. Divorce Statistics* as reported at www.divorcemagazine.com June 2003.

8. *National Vital Statistics Reports*, Department of Health and Human Services, National Vital Statistics System, Volume 50 Number 14.

ADDITIONAL RESOURCES

Whether you choose to seek a divorce or to try again on your marriage, it pays to be as informed as possible. There are numerous resources available to help you move forward in a constructive manner. Use them.

1. In local bookstores, look in the *self-help, self-improvement, and relationship sections*. For those of you who are readers, there are dozens of books about how to improve communication skills, how to improve your relationships, and how to maintain your marriage. Knowledge is power and you can learn how to change the status quo in your home.

2. Visit **local churches, classes, workshops and seminars**. Learning from books provides a great deal of information, but you need practice, too. Many mental health organizations, civic organizations, local colleges, and churches offer courses to improve your home life, sometimes at minimal cost. Take advantage of the opportunities there.

3. Visit the **National Domestic Violence Hot Line** at www.ndvh.org or 1-800-799-SAFE (7233). Physical abuse can be a problem that requires a serious commitment in order to be overcome. Both spouses must be committed to addressing this situation or be prepared to accept the consequences, which can be grave. This site has resources for both the victim and the perpetrator of abuse.

4. Another site to visit is the **National Vital Statistics System** at www.cdc.gov. The United States Center for Disease Control actually maintains statistics for all types of information, including marriage, divorce, children per family, unwed pregnancies, and other important data. The organization also releases articles that will help interpret the information and make it meaningful to you.

5. Read Sheehy, Gail, **Passages: Predictable Crises of Adult Life,** NY E.P. **Dutton, 1974**. This book will help you understand that the crises in your life may not be as unique as you think. May of us go through stages in adulthood similar to the stages of childhood, and our behavior is not necessarily unexpected, at least by those who are informed. Check out this book to see if your actions or those of your partner are part of the natural evolution of growth, rather than something that is extraordinary or unacceptable.

6. Read Stanton, Glenn, **Why Marriage Matters: Reasons to Believe in Marriage in Post-Modern Society, September 1977, Pinon Press**. This is an example of many books available that propose marriage is still a viable and vital institution in our society. If you do not believe in marriage in general, it may be hard to believe in your marriage personally.

7. **Contact state bar associations**. Every state has an association, usually in the capital city, which keeps track of the licensed attorneys in that state. Some states require attorneys to join the bar association while other states make it optional. A bar organization generally disciplines its lawyers and maintains records of complaints by the public. Certain types of discipline are private and others are public, meaning you can find out whether an attorney you are considering has had public discipline. It is like calling the Better Business Bureau for lawyers.

8. Contact your *state and local mental health facilities*. Every community has local mental health facilities and, often, state facilities. Some of these facilities are priced on a sliding scale, depending upon a client's income. Many individuals may require some additional assistance to learn how to communicate effectively. Some people have mental health issues precluding their ability to reason and communicate. Sometimes, these issues need to be addressed before a couple can work together constructively.

9. Visit *www.aamft.org* (American Association of Marriage and Family Therapy). This organization can assist in referrals for the type of therapist you may need. Remember that therapists are just people, and sometimes your personality may respond better to one therapist than another. You should try another therapist if you do not become comfortable with your first choice within a reasonable time. Sometimes people do not necessarily need therapy but instead need some life coaching skills. Coaching or mentoring is a new field and you should be cautious but open to new approaches in dealing with old problems. Finding the right coach for your marriage could make all the difference.

10. Visit *www.acresolution.org*. The Association for Conflict Resolution is a professional organization dedicated to enhancing the practice and public understanding of conflict resolution. This web site explains the mediation process in a family dispute setting and describes the attributes of a qualified mediator. It also has referrals for mediators registered with its organization.

11. Visit *www.divorcemagazine.com*. This site provides all sorts of useful information about divorce and about maintaining relationships. It has everything from Dr. Patricia Love's remarks, to call-in polls showing how many divorced people wish they had stayed married if they had known then what they know now. (A whopping 40%, by the way.)

12. Visit *www.marriagebuilders.com*. If you are willing to work on your marriage, this site will provide you with articles, workshops, information, and referrals to help you in that direction. There are a number of similar sites available, some of which are affiliated with universities.

13. Visit *www.mediate.com*. This site provides many interesting articles about mediation and the effects of divorce. It also has information regarding mediation training and a network of mediation and conflict resolution organizations throughout the country. A mediation referral service is available here as well.

14. Visit *www.nami.org* (National Alliance For The Mentally Ill). If you or your loved one is dealing with a mental health issue, you should be in contact with this organization. It may have resources available that will help you in ways you had not yet contemplated. A correct diagnosis is critical and, if not obtained, could explain why you feel like you are hitting your head against the wall.

15. Visit *www.smartmarriages.com*. This is another site that will provide a wealth of information and resources to help you save your marriage. This organization also has an annual seminar and provides training for individuals and therapists interested in assisting the rest of us work on our marriage. Remember, marriages, like any relationship, are rarely stagnant. They either get better or get worse; it is up to you. They do take effort but most people believe it is worth it.

CHILDREN'S BILL OF RIGHTS[7]

Children of divorce have the right to the following:

1
NOT TO BE ASKED TO "CHOOSE SIDES" BETWEEN PARENTS.

2
NOT TO BE TOLD THE DETAILS OF A BITTER, NASTY DIVORCE.

3
NOT TO BE TOLD "BAD THINGS" ABOUT THE
OTHER PARENT'S PERSONALITY OR CHARACTER.

4
TO PRIVACY WHEN TALKING TO EITHER
PARENT ON THE PHONE.

5
NOT TO BE CROSSED-EXAMINED BY ONE PARENT
AFTER VISITING OR TALKING WITH THE OTHER.

6
NOT TO BE ASKED BY ONE PARENT TO TELL
THE OTHER PARENT UNTRUTHS.

7
NOT TO BE USED AS A CONFIDANT REGARDING THE
DIVORCE PROCEEDINGS BY ONE PARENT OR ANOTHER.

8
TO EXPRESS FEELINGS, WHATEVER THOSE MAY BE.

9
TO CHOOSE NOT TO EXPRESS CERTAIN FEELINGS.

10
TO BE PROTECTED FROM PARENTAL WARFARE.

11
NOT TO BE MADE TO FEEL GUILTY
ABOUT LOVING BOTH PARENTS.

---

[7] *Office of the Guardian ad Litem, State of Utah.*